How To Play The Game For Business Success

Richard D. Connelly
Mark S. Grody

I play in many corporate and celebrity golf tournaments, and, being in the marketing business I see the value of meeting business people on the golf course and building business relationships there. **Corporate Golf** *offers easy-to-understand explanations and checklists to make sure you can get the most out of playing business golf.*
Bob Seagren, Olympic Gold and Silver Medal Winner

As the national sponsor of the annual Oldsmobile Scramble, involving more than one million golfers in the U.S., as well as sponsoring professional golf tournaments, we have learned the importance of planning, executing and evaluating each event. **Corporate Golf** *can be very helpful to any individual or company interested in building business relationships on the golf course. It all boils down to relationships, and this book is an outstanding guide on how to develop them over 18 very enjoyable holes of golf.*
Gus Buenz, Public Relations Director
Oldsmobile Division, General Motors

I see how the pro tournaments are run around the world, and nothing is left to chance. **Corporate Golf** *will help you leave nothing to chance!*
Lewis A. Yocum, M.D., Contributing Writer, Senior Golf
Kerlan-Jobe Orthopaedic Clinic, Los Angeles

CEOs, sales people...anyone who wants to do business on the golf course...should read this book. The tips are invaluable.
Warren Levy, President, Rawlings Golf

Corporate Golf:

How To Play

The Game

For

Business Success

Marketing Golf Resources
Los Angeles, California

Corporate Golf:

How To Play The Game For Business Success

By
Richard D. Connelly
Mark S. Grody

Published by
Marketing Golf Resources
P.O. Box 252097
Los Angeles, CA 90025 U.S.A.

ISBN 0-965 4995-2-9

Contents

Introduction

More than 20 million people in the United States alone play golf. Young, old, men, women — each has found a special reward in challenging the little white ball.

Whether you're a once-a-week or once-a-month recreational golfer or a "serious" golfer, you've endured the frustrations and relished in the joys that the game offers.

This "How To" book was written for all players who can look to golf as a way of building or enhancing business relationships. The "business of golf" is big business. Corporations spend millions upon millions of dollars annually sponsoring tournaments or individual professional players because they find business value in doing so.

You can find business value in golf, too. This book offers a "common sense, no nonsense" helpful approach to playing the game for business success.

Rick Connelly
Mark Grody

Chapter 1

Why Golf?

Eighteen holes of golf will teach you more about your foe than 18 years of dealing with him across the desk.

Grantland Rice

Why Golf?

Rewarding and frustrating, golf is a game that offers a sense of accomplishment, judgment, integrity, companionship and the challenge of competition. No wonder golf is played by major corporate executives and their colleagues throughout the world. In fact, there is hardly a business today that doesn't have either a direct or indirect tie to golf.

In many ways similar to business, golf is a "game" of mind and character, and after a few short hours on the course we form an everlasting opinion about our playing partners. It's an opinion that reflects not only on their personal lives, but also on their business strategies.

Many people play golf to enhance business relationships, but without playing with the "right" people, it can lead to a major disappointment in trying to build a business relationship.

You hear golf pros talk about course management as they play for success. Similarly, the corporate — or business — golf game must be played with a real purpose. In other words, have a business management plan when you play "business golf." If you don't have a game plan, you're in for a double bogey!

Golf has quite a reputation as providing an

arena for cutting a business deal. However, there's a right way and a wrong way to do business on the golf course.

To most people, the old quotation, "The deal was struck on the 17th hole," probably means the deal will land out of bounds!

Why? Because your golf game with a current customer or client is to enhance your business relationship. Your game with a potential customer is to create an atmosphere for building a strong business relationship. The office is the place to "do" the business.

Golf Talk

"The Ace"

A few years ago I was working at a well-known Los Angeles country club when a prominent celebrity member asked if I would play golf with him and the manufacturer of a product he endorsed. The celebrity was worried that the company executive was going to reduce or cancel the contract for his services, and he was anxious to preserve the relationship.

So, we established a business plan for the round of golf with careful consideration given to who would be the perfect member to fill out the foursome. The company representative was a poor player at best, but, by the end of the round, he had experienced his finest and most enjoyable round ever. While the executive's game was not his best, the companion-ship and collegial atmosphere within the foursome made the golf day successful.

A week later, the celebrity told me his contract was renewed for two more years. The round of golf with the company executive truly enhanced his business relationship, and the celebrity "aced" the business plan by being prepared, by having the "right" people in the foursome and by not giving a "hard sell" during the round of golf.

In this book, you'll learn how to prepare properly so your business golf outings will be "aces."

Chapter 2

Getting To The First Tee

Get a system of some kind in playing golf. Any

kind of system beats trusting luck.

Jack Burke, Jr.

Golf Talk

"The Par"

At a recent meeting with a major prospective retail account, we were reviewing our program proposal with a middle manager. The meeting had all the earmarks of a "courtesy visit," because our CEO had requested the meeting by contacting the prospective company's CEO.

As the meeting progressed, the retail manager was cold to our presentation, but he was listening because the CEO had asked him to do so. As the meeting ended, the manager said he would review our proposal with his boss.

I had just about counted out this visit as a lost cause when I asked, "Are there any golfers in this department?" The manager's eyes lit up, and he smiled, "We all play golf."

The door was now open, and I casually mentioned that I was a member of a prominent country club in the area. The manager said his boss once had a game scheduled there, but was rained out. The door opened a bit wider, and I suggested that we should give it another try some time with his boss.

He promptly introduced me to his boss, we talked about golf and agreed to a date. The first green was hit, and the business game was on!

Getting To The First Tee

"If you don't know the players, you won't have a successful golf game !"

Before you ever set up that first game of golf with a potential customer, you've got some work to do. Let's say your goal is to do business with the XYZ Electronics Corporation. The first thing to do is create your golf business plan.

In other words, you must know the company and its decision-makers — who in the company will buy your products or services? Then, selecting the business golf format becomes critical, so you need to do some research.

Get the answers to these questions:

- *Does the company stage any of its own corporate golf tournaments?*

- *Do any of your targeted executives play golf with your competitors?*

- *Do any of the executives play in industry tournaments? If so, which executives and which tournaments?*

- *Does the company sponsor a charity golf tournament?*

- *Are any of the company's executives members of country clubs?*

Your best source of information will be your

potential customer's "home course" — his office! That office is an indicator of his or her success and personal likes: trophies, books, awards, paintings, photos, magazines, etc. The decor will give you an idea of your customer's preferences.

This goes for all levels of the customer's home course — from the buyer to the CEO. Companies have business plans to pursue their sales objectives...and that means you need a business plan to attain your objectives, in this case the individuals you need to reach — whether it's the CEO, a buyer or some other individual.

Your responsibility in pursuing business golf is to know your potential customer's home course.

Ask the questions that will help you reach the first tee.

The Cold Call

Remember, business comes first, so during your initial meeting devote 90% of the time to listening to your prospective customer's needs and explaining how your product and services can fill those needs. The "other 10%" can be about recreation. This accomplishes your primary goal and sets the tone to build a future business partnership.

Ask the customer about his "home course" or what the company does for recreation. And, remember, let the customer do the talking. Listening carefully will help you get to know the player so you can organize your game plan.

If your prospect is not a golfer, he still can give you important information so you can prepare a secondary approach to building a business relationship. And, if the customer is a golfer...well, you know how a golfer likes to talk about the last six-foot putt that circled the cup and finally dropped!

Interpreting The Responses
Of Typical Golfers...

What You Need To Know!

"I play every week with my friends."

Find out where they play and if their friends are within the company.

"I like to play, but I never have time on the weekends."

Probably doesn't belong to a club, has a lot of personal and family commitments, but likes to play.

"I'd love to play golf, but work keeps me too busy."

Possible golf game on a weekend or holiday.

"The only time I play is in our company tournaments."

A comment you've been waiting to hear!!! The company's management is involved in golf. Don't be bashful — ask questions about the tournament.

"My boss and I play with vendors once in a while."

Pay dirt again...even if you don't like being called a 'vendor'! This person definitely wants a game! Find out where they play and if he and/or the boss is a member of a club. Remember again, golfers love to talk, so get that gleam in your eye and start asking questions: "What's your handicap?" "Where do you usually play?" And, throw in some comments about your own game and the courses that you play.

If it "feels right," invite the prospect to play golf then and there. If not, follow up and take the customer to a nice restaurant at a golf course. You can almost bet on it that your customer will give you a complete history of his game and of his company's involvement in golf. In other words, this is the conversation to "get the game flowing."

Don't forget, though, as you close your luncheon meeting, remind your customer about your

product and services, but leave the door open for

following up to arrange a golf game.

Getting To The First Tee Checklist

• Find out if your primary contact at the company plays golf.

• Learn if the top executives play golf.

• See if the company is involved in golf tournaments through sponsorship or other support.

• Determine whether your competitors play golf with your contacts or other company executives.

• If your main contact belongs to a country club, make sure you are familiar with it.

• Check to see if your customer or prospective client has a company policy about playing "customer golf."

• Leave the door open for a future golf game.

• Don't forget your business goal.

Chapter 3

Setting Up The Tee Time

Most golfers prepare for disaster. A good golfer

prepares for success.

Bob Toski

Golf Talk

"The Double Bogey"

A manufacturer's sales executive asked me to visit his company's out-of-state facility and discuss the possibility of purchasing some products. I accepted the invitation when I was able to combine the visit with other business in the same area of the country.

A week before the trip the national sales manager called me and suggested a round of golf after I had toured their plant. My schedule was tight, but like all good sales people he sold me on the game and assured me that I could stay on my schedule.

After the plant tour, we headed for a local country club. On the first tee I was astonished to watch my three manufacturer playing partners roll their drives an average of 100-150 yards. I spent the next 5 1/2 hours being a caddie looking for their lost balls.

By the fifth tee I found that the course was under construction, and we were going to play five temporary greens.

Between my shots and looking for lost balls, the three company representatives continually pressured me to take on their line. We finished the 18th hole in darkness and headed to the airport to catch my flight.

During the bumper-to-bumper traffic I again heard all the reasons why I should buy their products, how they meet all their production schedules and so on and so forth. Unfortunately, I was pre-occupied — the golf game was a disaster, and time was running short to catch my plane.

Needless to say, I was not in a "buying mood," and I certainly did not have any confidence in the company people I met. If they couldn't even handle the planning of a round of golf, how could I trust them with my business?!

Setting Up The Tee Time

It's probably not a very wise decision to walk into your first appointment with a prospective customer, introduce yourself and say, "How about a round of golf?" You need to prepare for that first round of golf, and you certainly don't want to give the impression that your business is all about play and nothing about work.

Just as you assess a customer's business needs so must you assess and evaluate the best way of setting up a golf match — and when to schedule that golf date. You need to evaluate the players and the best location to play.

Your customer needs time to talk to his business associates about your company and evaluate how you can provide him with the best product or service. Your "job" in that first business call is to lay the foundation for building a business relationship, although it's true that you might strike it lucky and make a sale during the first visit.

When you leave that first meeting you should have a feeling of confidence that you're an appropriate business supplier for the customer and that golf can play a strong role in developing a business relationship that will grow and prosper for years to come.

In looking at a follow-up to arrange a golf game, here are the things you need to consider:

1. Is your "target" a beginner or a seasoned player?

2. Does your customer have a "golfing buddy" or company colleague who could enhance your foursome?

3. Would it be an advantage to bring along an additional colleague from your company?

4. Should you invite a low handicap player to join your group?

5. What's the time of day and day of the week best suited for your prospect?

6. Where's the best location? If you're in your own home town and belong to a club, great. Consider your club or another setting which you can control (for example, a reciprocal club where you can gain access) and a "19th Hole" conducive to reviewing your round of golf and touching on some business.

7. If your prospect is located out of town, find a reciprocal club, a resort course or an excellent public course. In any case, do some research to find the best location.

Remember, review and offer the best possible scenario for your customer so you don't get a "not interested" response.

You must think about several variables depending on the skill level of the golfer you're inviting to play. You must make the customer feel comfortable with the golf environment you're providing. Here are some hints on setting tee times considering the handicaps of each player.

For the Beginner or High Handicapper

• Probably the easiest to impress with a golf game and the course of your choosing.

• Best location: a country club, resort golf course or excellent public course.

• Time of game: in the afternoon when play may be lighter; this takes the pressure off of playing fast.

• May need some education on the game of golf.

For the Seasoned or Mid-Handicapper

• Set the match for a country club or resort course which the customer hasn't played.

• Let the customer choose the time.

• The customer can help select the players for your foursome; maybe an "office buddy" will be asked to join you.

• Pick a golf environment where everyone will feel comfortable.

For the Low-Handicapper

This could be your toughest customer or prospect to please — on and off the course...or it could be one of the best experiences of all.

Keep the following in mind:

• Best location: your low handicapper usually will give you input, but you can be sure he'd prefer an excellent country club or a resort course.

• Let the customer set the time.

• The low handicapper usually likes "running the show" and, depending on the location, will want to fill out the foursome.

If he wants you to set up the foursome, consider the following:

1. Don't invite any beginners or high handicappers.

2. Bring along a colleague who is a solid player.

3. If need be, invite one of the course pros to join your group.

4. Golf etiquette is going to be very, very important.

5. If you are not a member of senior management, should you include such a person from your company?

6. The group should be compatible from a personality standpoint.

7. Should you have another low handicapper to balance out the foursome?

Once your date is set, stay in touch with your customer two or three times before game day. Now, your golf business plan is in the works!

Setting Up The Tee Time Checklist

- Remember to evaluate the players in your foursome; learn as much as possible about each player before the first drive is hit.

- Location, location, location — it's all-important to the success of this business venture.

- Time of day — don't forget about having lunch before you tee off...or refreshments and dinner after your round.

- Push for the most convenient time for your guests so they aren't interrupted during your round of golf.

- Make sure the players are compatible — by age, personality and handicap.

- This will be an "all play, no work" outing. Remember, your purpose is to build or enhance a business relationship, not ask for the order!

Chapter 4

Game Day

Focus not on the commotion around you, but on the opportunity ahead of you.

Arnold Palmer

Golf Talk

"The Bogey"

One of the more amusing — and ironic — experiences I remember before a golf game happened at an exclusive country club. A member had arranged for a foreign business executive to play as his guest. The guest arrived with some of his colleagues — wearing shorts. Through an interpreter, the pro shop attendant informed him that shorts were not allowed.

The executive decided to buy a new pair of pants, but, unfortunately, the pro shop had no pants that would fit — the pants were all too long, and the group's tee-off was 15 minutes away. One of the executive's colleagues unceremoniously "tailored" some new pants with him in them by cutting off the extra length. The guest strolled off to the first tee, and, yes, it was quite a sight to see!

As he hit a mulligan down the first fairway, he was again embarrassed when he was told that mulligans were not allowed. After the round he entered the clubhouse grill with his group for refreshments; the waiter asked him to remove his hat because hats where not allowed in the grill.

Now, in the whole scope of life on this planet, this is not a history-making event. But, it was an embarrassment for the visiting executive and his *member sponsor. Ironically, one early bird call by the sponsor's member or a business colleague could have saved a great deal of embarrassment.*

So, as the old Boy Scout motto says, "Be Prepared!!!"

Game Day
Checklist

"Game Day" finally arrives. The sun is shining, you're feeling great, you're ready to shoot your career round...and you're ready to enhance your business relationship the "right" way during the day.

Make sure to double-check everything so the experience comes off without a hitch.

- Be sure all the players understand the dress code before the round of golf. You don't want your guests to be embarrassed.

- Check with the course for any construction or

seasonal maintenance work; if there's a problem, change courses. You want this to be a completely pleasurable experience!

• As the host, make sure you get to the course a good hour before tee-off to set up everything. In other words, don't leave anything to chance...and don't make your business guest wait for you.

• Tell the pro shop, locker attendant and valet personnel that you have a guest coming so your guest will really feel welcome and be greeted properly.

• Plan for breakfast or lunch — make reservations if you need to; ask for a "view" table; ask for your favorite waiter and emphasize the importance of giving good service.

- Allow enough time to hit some practice balls on the range and to get a feel for the greens on the practice putting green.

- Give your guest some time in the pro shop; see if he spots something of interest — you might want to offer a souvenir.

- If you have golf balls with your company logo on them ... or a visor or something else with your company's identification on it, give your guest a sample or two.

- Determine the golf cart set-up. Who is going to ride with you? Make sure the person you "need to ride with" is the one who is with you in your cart. If you don't do this, you've lost a tremendous opportunity to build the relationship with your customer or potential customer.

- If you're playing at a public course, you must take the same careful approach so the game goes off without a hitch.

Chapter 5

The Game...
...And The Bets

Never bet with anyone who has a deep tan, squinty eyes and a one iron in his bag.

Dave Marr

Golf Talk

"The Shank"

A chemical manufacturer and I were working on a large retailer program, and after a successful meeting we talked ourselves into a golf game at my country club.

On the first hole, he promptly nailed his drive 275 yards down the middle, then claimed he was a scratch handicap. "Let's play a $10 Nassau...and we'll play even," he said. I must have looked shocked (actually I was dumbfounded) when he said: "Is the game too rich for your blood, or can't you win on your home course"? Now, make no

mistake, I've been hustled before, but not by a man-
ufacturer I brought in to pursue a mutually benefi-
cial business relationship.

Even though my opinion of him — and his
company — deteriorated, I accepted the challenge.
Not to my surprise, over the next several holes I felt
as if I was in a downpour because of all his crying
and whining about his game. That day he was as
close to being a scratch player as your pet dog or
cat!

After the front nine, I asked myself what would
happen if he ever lost a major deal like we were
working on that morning. Would he react to the
customer like he reacted on the golf course?

What resulted that day was a gallant effort to win some business being quickly destroyed by the embarrassing realization that my guest did not have enough money with him to pay his golfing debt.

The Game...And The Bets

"Yes, Virginia, there is a Santa Claus," and, yes, a lot of golfers enjoy a friendly wager or two during a round of golf. So, here's a red flag warning:

All the build-up of and for a business relationship can be destroyed before the balls are in the air by not knowing what to do about setting up a friendly wager!

If you're going to have a bet, make sure the amount is comfortable for the customer and for you. Remember, while it's not obvious, the customer is forming his opinion of you and your company.

Don't double bogey before you even leave the first tee!

Here are some guidelines:

With beginners or high handicappers, choose one of the following:

• Don't bet — "Let's go out and have some fun."

• Let's play for a drink after the round.

• Let's play two-against-two best ball within our foursome.

Also, remember:

• Keep all the bets the same, even if some players are regulars. Work the game to your advantage. In other words, if you need additional players for your foursome, think golf etiquette and business-building in your decision. Don't pick up players at the last minute to fill out your group.

With seasoned, low-handicap players, consider the following:

• Ask your guests what they'd like to play for.

• Either partner's best ball or skins is always a safe game.

• Don't let your ego get in the way of your wallet!

The Game...And The Bets
Checklist

- Set the game to have fun — you're not out to win the lottery or lose your house!

- Ask what your guest would like to do in the way of betting.

- Keep your bets within reason. Don't put any-one in the position of betting too much.

- Keep all the bets the same.

- Don't pick up players at the last minute to fill out your group...and your bets.

- Make sure all the bets are paid off.

- Remember golf etiquette.

Chapter 6

Balls in the Air

Start each hole with an awareness that there may be subtle or mysterious elements waiting to sabotage your game.

Robert Trent Jones, Jr.

Golf Talk

"The Triple Bogey"

A good friend of mine, Jack, a procurement manager for a major aerospace company, told me about a customer golf game that should have been an eagle but which turned into a triple bogey. A sales manager for one of the aerospace company's suppliers invited one of Jack's buyers to a golf game at a country club.

The sales manager suggested that the buyer bring along a friend to complete the foursome, and the aerospace buyer decided to invite his boss — my friend, Jack. The setting for the game was per-

fect, the bets were made, and balls were in the air.

Jack birdied the first hole en route to one of his best games ever. Unfortunately, the sales manager began to criticize and question Jack's handicap, and the sale rep's opportunities for business rapidly began going down hill.

Jack's game continued to improve, and he birdied the last hole to sweep all the bets. At the 19th Hole Jack said all drinks were on him to cele-brate his "career round." The bill easily exceeded his winnings, but he knew the "etiquette of winning" and paying for a round of drinks.

After a refreshment or two the sales manager rudely commented to Jack, "Does a sandbagger like you ever work for a living?" Unbelievably, the sales rep did not take the time to find out that Jack was his guest's boss!

Too late! The ball was in the hole, and Jack had formed an everlasting opinion of the sales rep and his company.

Lesson to be learned: "If you don't know the players, you can't play the game!"

Balls In The Air

Before the first ball leaves the first tee there is so much you can learn about the customer — and the customer about you.

Take a look at how your guest is dressed. What does his equipment look like? Compare it to being in the office — what does your guest wear in the office and what does the office look like? The answer — in the office and on the golf course — gives you a good idea about the level of importance placed on the meeting or golf outing. Your client's attire and accessories — as well as yours — set the framework for some good golf stories.

Take a look at the following:

- Is your guest wearing a visor, hat or golf shirt with his company's logo on it?

- What kind of clubs and bag does he have? Are they "garage sale specials" or does he take the game seriously?

- What about golf balls or a towel with a logo?

Be observant!

Your guest's first tee shot will give you an important clue in learning his general attitude for the game. You should set up your game to match his attitude. **For example, determine the following as soon as possible:**

- How serious is he?

- What's his speed of play?

- How's his eyesight — does he follow the ball or frequently lose sight of it?

- Is he nervous?

- How's his temper?

Remember, you are there to have the customer enjoy himself and be relaxed during the round of golf. So, you also may need to become a caddie!

- Watch your guest's game and where he hits his ball so you can help find balls that go astray.

- Help him with club selection.

- Advise him on distance/yardage to the hole, from the trap, etc.

- Help him line up his putts.

During pro-am golf tournaments, the pros play with the amateurs and still can maintain a quality game. You don't have to be the best golfer in the world, and you don't have to play your "career round" on the day you have your customer or prospective customer with you. **But you do need to do the following:**

- Don't complain about your game.

- No profanity.

- No cheating.

- No complaining about handicaps.

- Don't make business calls — leave your cellular phone and beeper in your car.

- Play at a steady pace.

- Remember the customer's good shots.

- Replace divots and repair ball marks on the green.

- Give information about the course and its history.

- Compliment good shots.

- Play competitively — you simply don't "let the customer win" to gain his business!

- Above all, keep your head in the business game!

The Customer Business Game Is On!

The first ball has been hit, and now you have that customer for the next four to five hours. Indeed, the game is on!

If you do your part, by the end of the round your customer will become a top supporter of you and your company. Like any investigator, you've done your research, and now you have all this time to interact with the customer.

Become a "pal," build that relationship which will last for many years to come. By the turn you should know a whole lot about your guest's personal life and business career.

Remember, keep the conversation focused on your customer or client.

During the round, the customer may bring up business because he might feel obligated to do so. But, here's a chance to make a birdie. Keep the business conversation to a minimum because there are too many distractions on the course.

If you've prepared the arrangements correctly, you'll have time to talk business after the round. Or, you can set a follow-up meeting at his office to further discuss or finalize a business deal. Either way, you've opened the door for the next meeting.

As you turn to play the back side, there is ample time for the customer to learn more about you. By the 10th hole the game should be getting into the "old buddies" mold with everyone having a great time, almost as if you've been playing together for years.

If you are not getting a positive response you have just bogeyed the first nine! If you can't turn it around in the next two hours, you just double bogeyed the complete game (start back at Chapter 1!). If the front side has been a birdie, you are now on your way to an eagle for the round.

The customer needs some information about you to build that relationship. If you've done your homework, you should have a whole bag full of data on his likes and dislikes, business goals and problems. Now is the time to show how some of your attributes complement his. But, don't "go for the jugular" — this is the time for subtle, soft-sell comments.

Balls In The Air Checklist

- Check out the customer's equipment.

- Determine the customer's golf attitude — will you have to "work" to have fun...or will this be a very serious day of golf?

- Have your company logo balls, hats or other mementos ready before you tee off.

- Make sure the cart partners are appropriate.

- Have an extra supply of balls in your bag.

- Watch the speed of play.

- Compliment the good shots.

- Be ready to buy a drink or sandwich for your group at the turn.

- Play your game within the rules.

- If you're a better golfer than your guest, don't give instructions or advice unless asked for it!

- Don't make business calls while you're on the course.

- **Don't "sell" on the course.**

Chapter 7

Playing In A Man's World

by

Nancy Oliver, *Founder*

Executive Women's Golf Association

Golf Talk

"Quadruple Bogey"

After hitting a 160-yard drive from the for-ward tee, Laura gingerly hopped back in the cart as her playing partner, Larry, proceeded to drive the cart directly to her ball. His ball was lying 30 yards ahead of her on the far right edge of the fairway. The other two in the foursome also were men, and their shots had found the right side of the fairway, too.

He took a few clubs and walked to his ball, leaving Laura with the cart while she prepared to shoot. After finishing her shot, she climbed in the cart and drove toward Larry when he finished his shot.

Larry dropped his club in the bag, walked to the driver's side and said, "Scoot over." Laura said, "That's okay, I'll drive." Larry insisted, "No, come on, really...scoot over." He was dead serious.

Two holes later, at the tee, Laura took her driver and walked towards the forward tee while the men prepared to tee off from the back tees. She stepped behind a tree while the three men teed off. Then Laura hit her drive, picked up her tee and walked toward the cart path only to watch both carts streak by her. Yes, Larry had forgotten about Laura. He came to a screeching halt about 50 feet *down the path, made a U-turn and came back to pick up Laura.*

No problem...it was an honest mistake. But, unfortunately, this happened again on three other holes. Larry forgot that his cart-mate — and business prospect — was teeing off from the forward tees.

Laura happened to be a buyer for a major department store chain, and Larry was trying to build a business relationship with her company because he manufactured products that he wanted to sell her. The only thing he sold her was an attitude of "why would I want to do business with someone as rude as Larry?"

There are dozens of revealing scenarios that emphasize the need for men and women to learn how to interact more effectively in a golf setting.

Larry had no clue...and no future business from Laura's company! A real quadruple bogey.

The information in this book applies equally to men and women, and golf can be as important a business tool to women as it has been to men for generations. So, it's important for everyone to understand that while the rules are the same — for men and women, in golf and in business — there are some situations that deserve special attention.

Playing In A Man's World
Checklist

- If you're hosting the outing, be sure to arrive at the course early enough to make the appropriate arrangements with the bag attendant and others.

- Let the bag attendant know who your cart-mate is going to be and that you'll do the driving. By driving, you'll be able to help control the speed of play.

- When the men tee off, stand on the tee with them so you can help spot the ball; have your cart-mate hit first. After they hit, head for the cart and drive to the ladies tee...with your club selection already made.

- Help look for lost balls; everyone in your foursome should do so; no exception for ladies!

- Statistics show that about 85% of all men have a wager of some kind during a round of golf. If you're going to take part, be sure you understand how the game works.

- Regardless of how high or how low the stakes are, you should get all the details before you're in the thick of it.

- Don't bet if you don't feel comfortable doing so.

- NEVER bet what you can't afford to lose!

- Mentally keep track of your score on each hole. There's nothing worse than holing out your last putt, looking back at the hole and spending two minutes trying to remember how many strokes you had.

- No two people hit exactly the same distance with the same club. Make your club selections without worrying about — or asking — "what did you use on that shot?" The club that your male partner used has nothing to do with your swing. How you choose to play the hole is up to you.

- Make a decision and stand behind it confidently.

You do it in business ...

do it on the golf course!

Chapter 8

The 19th Hole

Management — placing the ball in the right position for the next shot — is 80% of winning golf.

Ben Hogan

Golf Talk

"The Lost Golfer...

...Definitely In The Hazard!"

After a great round of golf at a supplier's country club, the member invited three of us who worked for the same company and who were his guests to the 19th Hole for refreshments, a re-hash of the day's events and settling up of bets. The camaraderie among the group was perfect, topping off a wonderful round of golf in which the best ball bet was halved with great birdies on the 18th hole.

Now, you know how golfers are — they don't know the meaning of the phrase, "To be immortal you don't have to be eternal"! In other words, they like to talk...and talk...and talk — about that down-hill, 15-foot putt that lipped out on number six, the three-wood that cleared the water on number 12 and landed on the green in birdie territory and the duck hook into the trees on number 13.

The typical dialogue involves a lot of "what ifs" and "if onlys." There's no such thing as a "short" story in recounting a round of golf. And, as the story-telling continues, the drink glasses are likely to get empty and re-filled several times.

After two hours of competing for bragging rights, along with a number of "refreshments," the member invited us to stay for dinner. Everyone was having a great time, and before we knew it, the four of us had agreed to continue our match the next morning.

There was no problem because our flight out wasn't until later the next day. So, the socializing continued, and after a long and exhausting day, we decided to call two "designated drivers" — taxicabs — one to take our member/host home and the other to take my colleagues and me to the hotel.

The first cab arrived, and we jumped in and headed for the hotel. The member waited for the second cab.

The next morning we arrived at 6:30 a.m. and were impressed that our member/host was ready to go; the carts were loaded up; the sun was already shining; and the first tee beckoned.

We did notice, however, that our host was wearing the same outfit he wore the previous day...only with a few more wrinkles in his pants and shirt than before! But, nobody mentioned anything, and very quickly we were on the way down the first fairway.

Later, as we approached the 18th green, we saw the member's spouse standing behind the green. We putted out, said hello and headed for the showers to clean up.

As we were dressing, the member walked in, wearing an embarrassed grin. He sheepishly explained that the night before he had decided to sit in his car and wait for the taxi. Yes, he fell asleep and woke up just before we arrived for our match.

He tried to call home to apologize to his spouse, but there was no answer. She was out searching for her husband, the "lost golfer."

Moral of the story — have fun, but watch what you drink. Watch out for each other, and don't drive when you've had too much to drink. You don't want to end up in a hazard that you will never get out of.

The 19th Hole

After four or five hours on the golf course, prolonging the day's experience and moving it into a business environment becomes important. How you plan your golf game time translates into how you will keep the meeting ongoing in a productive manner.

Remember, it's better to golf and then relax — not eat and then play if you expect to maximize your business opportunity. For example:

- A morning round can extend into lunch where you can talk business.

- A mid-day round can extend into refreshments and appetizers.

- A late-afternoon round means an extension into refreshments — and maybe dinner.

Obviously, there's always the possibility of the customer running out of time because of other business or personal commitments. If that's the case, the next step must be quick and to the point. If the customer must leave, and you are saying your good-byes, reaffirm the good time had by all and set up a time for a follow-up appointment.

Don't try to give a sales pitch while your customer is trying to leave!

Don't waste the opportunity of making a "fast pitch" or "wasted pitch" when your customer or client is in a hurry.

If you have played a late golf round and dinner is a possibility, there are some things you should consider. If the clubhouse has a casual attire policy, all is fine, but if you need to leave the club, problems could arise. Many — if not most — golfers don't like to finish a round, shower, put on a coat and tie and head off to a fancy restaurant. If possible, keep things on track at your golfing location.

Be sure to let the customer give you some insight in the matter. You may have eagled the golf game, but you have another one or two hours to bogey the dinner! Remember, too, the later it is, the less the customer will want to discuss business.

So, in most cases, the ideal times for a game are morning and mid-day rounds. Why? To give you maximum selling time.

After you finish your round, sit down and talk about the highlights on the golf course. Maybe there only were one or two good shots or one long putt that dropped, but your customer (or prospect) — like all golfers — likes to review the day's golfing accomplishments and the "what-ifs" (e.g., *If only I hadn't missed that three-foot putt on number 16!*).

Remember, your customer also must be reminded that you had a great day hosting him! It's okay to let the customer lead that part of the conversation. At any rate, you should receive some "signals" relating to the day's events and the prospect of further developing the business relationship.

In fact, many times, if you've *eagled* the round of golf, your customer will suggest a follow-up business meeting. If you've *parred* the golf round *YOU* need to set up the next meeting.

It's important to remember that you don't have to close a deal right then and there. It's more important to enhance your overall business relationship.

Remember, too, that some great business golf games have been destroyed in the 19th Hole because of one too many drinks. When a problem occurs it haunts the business partnership for all parties.

Check the scoreboard to evaluate your business golf game.

The 19th Hole
Checklist

- Talk about the good shots.

- Pay off the bets.

- Keep in mind that your guest may be on a tight schedule and might need to leave promptly.

- Don't let the customer do all the talking; carefully weave your business plan for the day into the conversation.

- Keep all the players in the conversation.

- Don't over-sell — set up the next call.

- Don't "over party."

- Remember to tell your guest about the great time you had together during the round of golf.

Chapter 9

The Scoreboard

A bogey can be like a wake-up call — it can snap you back mentally.

Peter Jacobsen

Golf Talk

"What Was My Score?"

Many — if not most — companies have that "super sales manager" who inspires customers to buy their products or services. Our company's super sales manager set up a morning meeting with a major, large-volume customer, followed by an afternoon round of golf.

The day started with a thorough meeting to review our services and to assist in some additional problem areas. The meeting resulted in additional product sales for us as well as instituting a training program for the customer's employees. Definitely an "eagle" meeting!

We had invited the president of our company and our local rep to lunch to get better acquainted with the customer. The customer was extremely impressed with our management and also talked about how much he was going to enjoy playing golf at our club. **Score a birdie!**

The set-up for the game was in place, and as our customer reached his cart, he found a club logo shirt and hat...and waiting on the cart was his playing partner — our president. Being a four handicap our customer was presently surprised to find that the highest handicap in the group was a 12, and he commented on how much fun this was going to be. **Score a birdie!**

On the third hole our "super sales manager" lost his business game by his constant profanity, and he managed to "air mail" a few clubs along the way after bad shots. The customer asked me, "Does he get this way all the time?" I assured him he was very competitive and was a true winner. The only problem after that statement was that, on the next hole, we both were unbelievably shocked to see him cheating. **Score: double bogey.**

At the turn the super sales rep was beeped by the home office and, because of an unexpected problem, our president had to bail out. **Score: a definite bogey.**

Nonetheless, the golf game continued with the customer enjoying the course and commenting how he would appreciate playing with us again. At the 19th Hole he took over the conversation and repeatedly told us how much he appreciated our company's commitment to giving his company the best possible service. **Score: ace!**

A week later I called on the customer to follow up on the programs we instituted for his company. The super sales manager had failed to meet his commitments, but the local representative had satisfied his present needs. The customer requested that even though the super sales manger was a friend, he would like to coordinate all activities through the local rep. **Score: par.**

Our business with the customer continued to grow through the local rep, and we still play golf a few times a year as friends. **Score: eagle.**

The Scoreboard

The scoreboard relates directly back to your initial golf and business plan for the customer you are targeting. While the purpose of the game is to build the relationship the key is the development of the business between your company and your potential customer's firm?

Here's how to score your success:

Ace or Double Eagle

- The customer has agreed to buy your product or service or has approved of doing business together.

Eagle

- The customer has given you an initial order on a trial basis.

Birdie

- The customer is setting up additional meetings with some of his colleagues and will totally support your position as an approved supplier.

Par

- You have set up a meeting with the decision-makers but have not received a commitment.

Bogey

- Your guest politely says he'll "check out" the appropriate people for you to talk with and will call you back.

Double Bogey

• After four or five hours together you don't get an additional meeting, and you don't know what you did wrong!

The scoreboard provides an evaluation of your complete business golf plan. An eagle or birdie is a great score, par or bogey may lead to a better score. Double bogey means that you have just hit a ball out-of-bounds, and that may have been created by inviting the wrong player, or it may have been your overall performance.

Scoreboard
Checklist

Evaluate the overall performance. Look for future ways to improve the way the day went.

- Was the customer a prime contact for future business dealings?

- Did the golf course meet the expectations of your guest?

- Did the time of day work for your customer?

- Were all the players compatible?

- Will you be asked to take part in the customer's company golf activities?

- Did you score well on your golf business plan?

Chapter 10

Corporate Golf Tournaments

Golf is a thinking man's game. You can have all the shots in the bag, but if you don't know what to do with them, you've got trouble.

Chi Chi Rodriguez

Golf Talk

"The Eagle"

Earlier in my career when I was working for a national service company, a sales manager who recently began calling on a large supermarket chain asked me how we could get further into the mainstream of the company.

The chain had an invitational company tournament for management and large volume suppliers. But, frankly, the event was too rich for our budget. We did find out that the company had district tournaments for all employees and local support vendors. With the help of a store manager we *entered our first tournament.*

We knew from past experience an important point not to overlook: instead of entering as a foursome we would enter as a twosome to give us a better opportunity to play with people from the chain. We arrived at the tournament and were paired with a food vendor, which turned out to be very fortunate for us.

Besides having a great day on the course, our playing partners provided information on who plays in the tournaments, and how the vendors use the tournaments to their advantage. In fact, we found that our biggest competitor played in every district event.

After the round of golf, we watched suppliers donate products and gifts to a raffle. We asked our sales rep if he had donated a prize, but he had failed to do any research and contributed nothing. Our competitor proudly delivered a prize to the raffle table, and that left us with three options: no prize donation; go to the pro shop and buy something to donate; or develop a high-impact donation.

We chose the latter, and on the back of a business brochure we literally created an on-the-spot impact donation — a prize of golf and lunch for three at my country club. When I approached the person running the raffle, I briefly explained the prize and where the club was located.

The person running the raffle was good at des-ignating the donor of each prize. Number after number was called, but our donation was not to be seen or heard from. At the end of the drawings, the raffle organizer stated, "Today's grand prize is a golf and lunch outing for three at a country club."

Not only did he mention the name of our com-pany as having donated the prize, but he also explained what services and products we per-formed for his company. The winner turned out to be a corporate manager for the chain. After dinner I went to the manager and explained that he could call me to set up the game, and that I would be play-ing in the foursome as his host.

As I made my way through the dining room thanking the golf tournament organizers and introducing myself to everyone, I noticed that my competitor's foursome was sitting alone not interacting with the group. On the other hand, our company now had become associated with the sponsoring company as the firm which donated the great grand prize.

Thereafter, our firm continuously received invitations to all of their company's tournaments, and while we were playing with different groups, our competitors were playing their same company foursome, not taking advantage of enhancing any business relationship.

Business moral of the story: "If you are going to play the game, get the recognition, and make it work for you."

Corporate Golf Tournaments

Every Monday, corporate America tees off with company golf tournaments. In fact, in recent years, the tournaments have expanded to almost every day of the week. Companies and industry organizations have added golf to their annual functions almost as a matter of course.

Companies use these events to bring together employees, prospective customers, current vendors and other individuals important to the company to interact in a relaxed atmosphere. These firms truly do use golf for building and maintaining solid business relationships.

Companies that do not conduct their own tournaments should look closely at taking part in tournaments run by other companies. By adding golf to the overall business budget a company can receive a great deal of effective exposure at a minimum cost. The impact of your name at the tournament will be seen by all the players and support groups.

Getting On The Tourney Tour

The typical company tournament chairperson is looking for your support — as a golf participant, a prize donor or in some other fashion — but he doesn't always know where to find you or your company. That chairperson is involved with the inner circles of his company and can eventually benefit your company. Finding that person and the events that are appropriate for your company may take some research, and there are some logical places to look:

• Company newsletters.

- Flyers posted on bulletin boards at company offices.

- Purchasing office.

- Personnel office.

- Vendors.

- Industry trade publications.

- Word of mouth.

Golf tournaments can be birdies or bogies! At all golf tournaments the more gifts or prizes the players receive, the more successful they will rate the tournament. The course or format may be a bogey, but if the player leaves with a prize it can well be a birdie.

When approaching the tournament's chairperson, identify your firm and ask how you can support his company's efforts. You'll surely get a positive reaction from the chairperson, because he is anxious to have your support and will give you plenty of ideas on how you can participate.

For example, you could provide some of the following prizes:

- Golf balls.

- Towels.

- Hats or visors.

Don't forget your company logo on these items!

You could offer other prizes too, such as:

- Golf equipment.

- Tee sponsorship.

- Trips.

- Cash.

- Samples of your product if appropriate.

Tournament chairpersons will be most appreciative of anything you can offer, and they will cooperate to ensure that you get the proper identification and credit.

Your first conversation with the tourney chairperson will give you excellent insight on the importance of the tournament. Tell the chairperson that you will call him back to let him know what your commitment will be.

Why? This allows you time to set up your business plan and consider the following:

• How much exposure do we need?

• Can the chairperson support my efforts to do business with his company?

• How are your competitors supporting the tournament, if at all?

• Is the tournament open to all vendors?

The justification for your participation and gift contribution must be determined by the impact of your future ability to gain entry into their business. Also, keep in mind that if the tournament is open to other vendors, they always have a chance of winning too.

Some high impact prizes to consider are:

- Logo balls.

- Logo towels.

- Logo hats or visors.

- Tee sponsorship.

There are low impact prizes, too, and they would include the following:

- Non-logo golf equipment.

- Your product, unless it very unique and useful.

- Cash.

- Trips.

- Gift certificates.

You should look for exposure in one of two ways:

1. The fact that you associate and involve your company — by name — with an appropriate tournament; or,

2. You're providing a memorable prize that every player wants; one that makes executives and other participants compliment you about the prize.

The second might sound expensive, but it can be relatively inexpensive and pay off handsomely by building the future relationship you are looking for within a target company. The chairperson of the tournament wants to make sure his top management looks at the event as being successful.

So, he may direct your prize to one of his top executives. The chairman wants your support for next year and may "plant his own seeds for your future involvement" by being very cooperative in giving you the exposure you desire before the people you need to reach. Here are some "business building" prizes:

- A round of golf and lunch for three at an exclusive club or resort.

- Putters with the company's logo on it.

- A weekend trip to an exclusive club or resort.

- Golf bag with the company's logo.

If the winner is another vendor, look at it as an opportunity to obtain vital information that can be helpful to your company.

When returning the call back to the chairperson with your company's donation, be sure to ask the chairperson if someone from your company can play in the tournament. If the tournament is open to vendors you can see your plan in action. If the tournament is not open to vendors you still can gain insight on how to approach their company to establish or enhance a business relationship.

Whether you play in the tournament or not you must evaluate your participation for future consideration. Like trade shows there are good and bad tournaments, but if you don't play you won't even have a chance to get up to bat for some business!

Playing the Tournament

If the chairperson invites you to play, don't get locked into a foursome consisting only of players from your company; try to have one or two players play in different groups. This gives you the opportunity to play with the customer or with vendors who can give you important information on the customer or the industry. By "spreading your-selves out," you can more than double your effec-tiveness.

Tournament Game Day

You may be a guest, but this tournament is an introduction of your company. In other words, "the business game is on." Take a short time to say hello to the chairperson, but keep it short because he will be very busy.

A gift to your foursome — perhaps logo golf balls or hats — can start the game in the right direction. Even if it is another vendor in your foursome, you want to emphasize that your company is a player in the business game.

During the social hour after the game thank the chairperson on the great day that your company had and tell him that you would enjoy participating next year. Most teams sit together at dinner. If, for some reason your teammates don't stay for dinner, don't sit alone! Look for a table that also has other players.

In fact, for the most benefit, here again you and your company colleagues should split up at dinner — this multiplies your chances to meet people, some of whom may be prospective customers.

Be a good listener at dinner. What you hear from company employees, vendors and others at your table can be very helpful to you and should be a critical part of your golf business day.

Keep an eye out for the "business players" — the people you need to know inside the company. Make a point to meet them, and also watch their reactions during the awards presentation. If your prize is part of the event, assess the interest those key players have in your gift and others.

After the awards presentation introduce yourself to the winner and make arrangements for a time to plan out the prize, if you've contributed a round of golf, for example.

Like any trade show review the program for future consideration.

Corporate Golf Tournaments Checklist

- Find the tournaments.

- Know the tournament chairperson.

- Allocate budget to play in key customer/corporate tournaments.

- Donate some important prizes.

- Learn from other vendors.

- Play by the rules of golf and golf etiquette.

- Stay for the awards banquet.

- Thank the organizers for a great time.

- Make an impact for your company.

- "Plant seeds" for future involvement.

- Leave the tournament knowing more about your customers than before you started.

Chapter 11

Your Company Golf Tournaments

Great champions have an enormous sense of

pride. The people that excel are those who are dri-

ven to show the world — and prove to themselves

— just how good they are.

Nancy Lopez

Golf Talk

"A Par"

For years, I played in a golf tournament run by a company sales rep. The tournament was open to all employees, vendors and a few selected customers.

Because the tournament was open to all employees the tournament needed to be on a weekend, and that raised the expense. Plus, there was a problem finding a course that could accommodate the company. Participants were from all handicap groups and represented many cultural backgrounds.

The sales rep did an excellent job of securing a

centrally located public golf course. However, because of the course, this tournament, with more than 72 players, was limited to tee times. That created a 2 1/2-hour gap from the first group finishing to the last group sinking their last putt.

The company's upper management always elected to play early so they could finish and leave. The vendors and sales personnel never got a chance to rub elbows with the management. Also, the players who finished early had a simple question to ask: "What do I do for the next couple of hours before the awards presentation?"

It's true that the awards presentation and accompanying raffle was an event to look forward to because of the great gifts and the fact that everyone won something. The sales rep did an outstanding job in obtaining prizes, many of which were from the company's vendors, but keep in mind that the vendors need a "payback" too. They'd appreciate the opportunity to interact with management who may support their cause inside the company.

The tournament was always a great event, and the chairperson was outstanding, but the commitment was for a 12-hour day...and management didn't keep their part of the bargain!

Remember, "Keep the game flowing, so that all will enjoy the experience."

Your Company Golf Tournaments

Preparing for your own company golf tournament is similar to developing a business plan. The effort that is placed into the work on hand — and not forgetting the "small details" — will create the ultimate success of the event.

A company tournament or outing can include as few as 12 to more than 100 players, depending on the scope of the program.

Your business is a professionally run organization, dedicated to being successful. The same attitude and careful planning and execution must be maintained in any company golf project, whether it's a large tourney or a sales outing.

You must appoint a chairperson. Planning a tournament by committee will lead to a bogey at best. In every company, there must be a boss who takes responsibility for the event. Just as good sales reps don't always make good managers, it holds true that all good golfers don't always make good tournament chairpersons.

Too often they set the game for their benefit and not for the enjoyment of all the players. Keep in mind that the average golfer is really lucky to break 100!

The tournament can have a great golf course, all the right players, the correct match-ups, prizes and format, but if the chairperson is unorganized, it reflects back to your general approach to conducting business. Look for the following qualities in selecting an ideal chairperson:

- Excellent organizer.

- Very detail-oriented.

- Golf experience.

- Excellent communicator.

- Persistent.

- Solid vendor relationships.

The Tournament Players

With the chairperson in place, the company must decide on its general business involvement and the employees who will participate. Having the "right" people involved can make or break the event.

Here are the groups of people you must consider:

- Customers.

- Levels of customer management to be invited.

- Which of your executive management team will participate?

- What other levels of management will take part?

- Other employee involvement.

- Which vendors will you invite?

- What levels of vendor management will you invite?

- What special employee guests will be invited?

A decision must be made about the participants in the tournament and the pool of available players. The chairperson then can formulate a golf tournament plan and budget to achieve the expectations of the tournament. If customers are a factor, all plans must be developed with them in mind.

Day and Date

The makeup of the players and the number of participants will determine the location and time of your event. The tournament could be in tandem with another corporate or industry function which, obviously, would simplify the date. If that is the case careful research of the schedule of events will help set up your game day.

If the tournament is for all comers, participation could be a problem. Weekday locations are easier to fit into your schedule, while weekend and holiday tee times could become a difficult task. But, weekdays also take customers, management, vendors and employees out of the work environment.

Always keep in mind the seasonal weather elements. What happens if it rains? Have an alternate plan in mind — perhaps lunch with an indoor "clinic" from the club pro, followed by large-screen TV showings of U.S. Open highlights or some other appropriate video.

Location

Once your chairperson has an approved date the location becomes the factor. The players and the budget will cause you to consider the following:

- Customers.

- Management.

- Number of players.

- Skill levels.

- Vendors.

- Employees.

- Convenience of location.

- Availability of banquet facility.

If customers are to be your players, the chairperson must upgrade the location, and that means it will cost more. The quality of your tournament equates to the quality of the product or service you sell. If your company prides itself on its high quality, make sure the tournament is of equally high quality.

If top management and vendors are the players, management should lend support in the location decision. If the tournament is for all comers, the skill level of the players is all-important for the location of the tournament. If most of your guests are higher handicap players, you definitely don't want to choose the toughest course. You want people to enjoy the round with a fair, but challenging layout.

Location: Customers And Management

Resort or semi-private golf courses usually are waiting for your functions (if they already are not seeking them out on their own) and have sales representatives and staff to support your needs. In many situations if the course has 36 holes or more, weekend times will be available. Country clubs usually have time available on Mondays which have become more or less traditional days for corporate and charity tournaments.

Location: All Players

Budget is going to play a significant role in your course selection. In many situations a company will have the players pay for their green fees and cart fees, with the company covering the cost of a lunch, dinner, reception or other awards ceremony. If this is the case, don't over-price the tournament. There are excellent public golf courses that will satisfy your needs.

Once you have a location idea or two in mind, the chairperson should discuss the possibilities with other golfers in the company. An in-person visit is a necessity to meet the course representatives, make the arrangements and paint a solid picture in your mind of how the tournament day will take place. And, very importantly, the people who "book" tournaments at the course you select will give you excellent ideas based on their own knowledge and experience. Remember, too, they want to sell their program to your company.

Time of Day

If your group is small (under 20 players) tee times usually are acceptable. Anything over 20 and you'll require a shotgun start.

Don't forget, with five tee times for 20 people, there will be a "lapse time" of nearly an hour. The first group will have completed its round and will be waiting for the last group to finish. A shotgun start lets all players start and finish together, and your plans for the awards presentation or meal will not be prolonged.

The exact time of the start must be best suited for your overall tournament plan. If it is a corporate outing during a conference or a trade show, your tournament starting time should not conflict with other functions.

If the tournament is on a business working day, a mid-day start is ideal. Players can get some work done before heading out to the course. A weekend or holiday time can be arranged so no work time is lost, but such an event could interfere with family or other plans.

Remember, if you start your tournament at mid-day, allow about 5 1/2 hours to complete the round.

Arrival at the Tournament

You only get one chance to make a good first impression, so make sure that as people arrive at your tournament, they are greeted and signed in appropriately.

You should have arrangements made for a bag drop so players can unload their cars before parking them (unless there is valet parking). A "Welcome" sign is always a good touch.

A registration area should be clearly marked, and the tournament chairperson and company executives should be there to greet the players. Nothing is better than having your company president welcome all the players as they arrive.

When the players register, they should be given their tee prizes (a small pack of appropriate items — e.g., tees, balls, towel), a set of the rules and clear directions on where to proceed.

Golf Tournament Format

Pairings

No matter what format you choose, try your best to have a company representative in each foursome (or fivesome). Remember, you're sponsoring this event to cultivate and enhance business relationships, and the more interaction you can have between your company officials and your guests, the more successful the event will be.

Most importantly, you must do your best to make sure all the players both enjoy their golf experience and that they finish in a timely manner. There are several tournament formats you can choose for your event, such as the following:

Scramble

- *Advantages*

    - Easy to score.

    - Mix low and high handicaps in the same foursome.

    - Encourages team work.

    - Allows all players to be involved.

    - Everybody can contribute to the team's success.

- *Disadvantages*

    - Difficult to handicap.

    - Some players prefer the challenge of only playing their own ball for 18 holes.

Two Low Balls: Net or Gross

- *Advantages*

    - Players can pick up when they're "out of the hole."

    - Pure team effort.

    - Mix in high and low handicaps.

- *Disadvantages*

    - All players need to be handicapped.

    - Scores need to be checked.

    - Complete pairings required.

Individual Stroke Play

- *Advantages*

  - Easy to score.

  - No problem if you have "no shows."

- *Disadvantages*

  - All players need a handicap.

  - Slower pace of play.

If you have a mixed group of golfers — low handicaps, high handicaps and no handicaps — besides awarding low net and gross prizes, you should consider a "Callaway" scoring as an alternative for the high and no-handicappers who play in the tournament. A Callaway system provides an equitable way for such players to compete on an even basis, and the scoring will be done by the pro shop.

At the check-in area and on each cart be sure to have a printed sheet which explains the tournament format and the rules. You want to be certain that all players understand the game.

With a shotgun start, one of the course pros should explain the rules before teeing off, and this usually is done after all players have settled into their carts. If the tournament is "tee time" format, the pro should be on the first tee to explain the game.

Remember, scoring takes time, and the golfers will be anxious to hear the results. You should arrange with the pro shop to assist you with

all the scoring.   You also should pass out printed

results so all the participants can see the complete

list of the standings and how they fared.

Awards Presentation/Banquet

The awards presentation or banquet should be set up in a timely manner after the last players finish. That coordination is extremely important with the staff of the golf course to keep things running smoothly.

Keep in mind that your participants will have been at the course for five to six hours, and if you over-extend that period for another two or three hours, the day has become much too long. Like the golf game, you need the awards portion of your event to flow. Otherwise, you could birdie the golf game and double bogey the awards presentation.

Your Golf Tournament Checklist

- Pick the right chairperson.

- Select the players.

- Determine the budget.

- Pick the "right" location and date.

- Pick the right time of day.

- Choose the best tournament format for the group.

- Pick out memorable prizes and awards.

- Have an alternative plan if you have to call off the tournament because of bad weather.

- Determine the timetable and the extent of food and beverages you will supply.

- Make sure to have a well-planned awards presentation.

- In advance, notify all players of the dress code.

- Give all players a schedule of events and a map to the course.

- Make sure the golf course personnel can support your program.

- Be sure your staff is prepared to handle all the activities "without a hitch"?

Chapter 12

Etiquette

Golf puts a (person's) character on the anvil and his richest qualities — patience, poise and restraint— to the flame.

Billy Casper

Golf Talk

"Etiquette"

In the last 30 years the game of golf has improved dramatically — in golf courses, equipment, fashion and knowing the rules, but, unfortunately, the etiquette of the game often falls by the wayside.

When I started playing golf as a teenager at a country club, I learned golf etiquette very quickly! I was playing alone when a member who was a good friend of our family asked me to join his threesome. On the first hole I sunk a miracle 70-foot putt and left the ball in the hole as the group putted out.

As we walked down the next fairway the member explained — firmly — that I did not show proper etiquette on the first green because I left my ball in the cup. He also "lectured me" about the importance of etiquette throughout the game.

Under my breath I was calling him a bad name or two. But, what I did not understand at the time was that he had just given me the ultimate playing lesson.

While golf may mostly be an individual sport, your opponents, partners and guests are affected by your play and your etiquette. While good scoring is determined by your ability (and sometimes some good luck), your own good etiquette is always determined by you and your actions alone.

Etiquette

According to Webster's, the definition of etiquette is: "conventional requirements as to proper social behavior; a prescribed or accepted code of usage in matters of ceremony; the code of ethical behavior among members of a profession."

In golf, as in business and your personal life, there is etiquette, and **YOU MUST KNOW GOLF ETIQUETTE IF YOU ARE TO PLAY THE GAME**. Each year the United States Golf Association (USGA) prints a new, updated version of the Rules of Golf. How important is etiquette to the USGA?

In the Rules of Golf, the first subject addressed is etiquette — before any discussion of rules and definitions.

The USGA cannot define every minute detail of etiquette. But, the overriding thought is that golf is a game that involves discipline, accomplishment, judgment, integrity, companionship and the challenge of competition...so, play it with character.

The Rules of Golf also are very important, and the USGA and The Royal and Ancient Golf Club of St. Andrews explain extensive rules and definitions. You don't have to know all the details of all the rules and definitions, but you should be sure to know the basic rules and definitions.

Similarly, in the business world, a sales representative may not need to know every nut and bolt about how his company's product is engineered, but he definitely needs to know the features and benefits of that product or service.

Here are some important points about etiquette to remember.

Courtesy on the Course

Safety

- Before taking a practice swing or hitting a shot, make sure that nobody is standing close by or in position to be hit by your club, the ball or any stones, pebbles, twigs or other things that might be moved when you swing your club.

- Yell "FORE" loud and clear if you hit a ball in another person's direction.

- Watch your temper — throwing a golf club in anger isn't going to improve your game...and it could be dangerous.

- Golf cart accidents can happen; be sure to drive the cart by the rules...and use common sense.

Consideration For Other Players

- The player who has the honor (the one with the lowest score on the previous hole) should be allowed to hit first.

- Don't move, talk or stand close to or directly behind the ball or the hole when a player is addressing the ball, swinging a club or putting.

- Don't drive your cart or walk ahead of other players before they hit their shots.

- Keep an eye on the ball when the other players in your group hit; they may need help finding their balls.

- Don't hit your ball until the players in front of you are out of range.

- Don't walk in another player's line on the green — in other words, don't step in between a player's ball and the cup because you could affect the roll of the ball with your spikes.

- After putting, take your ball out of the hole with your hand — don't use your putter; it could damage the cup.

- Don't yell to each other — remember there are other players on the course trying to concentrate on their shots. Etiquette in your foursome applies to all players on the course.

- If you're playing bad, don't over-complain; it affects your fellow players.

Pace of Play

- Is there anything worse than getting behind a group that takes an eternity to hit the ball? In the interests of all players, be sure to play without delay!

- Be ready to hit your shot; don't wait until your turn to pick a club or line up a putt.

- If your group doesn't keep up with the group in front, and you're holding up the group behind you, let the group behind you play through.

- If you're looking for a ball, signal the players behind you to play through as soon as it becomes apparent that you're not going to find your ball easily. In all cases, do not look for more than five minutes before waving the next group through. Then, let that group get out of range before you resume play.

- When the last person in your group has putted out, leave the green immediately.

- Drive or walk to the next tee before writing down scores, cleaning your club or otherwise "dallying." In other words, get out of the way — promptly!

Care of the Course

• Rake the sand trap before you leave it — that means fill in any holes and footprints you've made — plus others that someone else neglected to fill.

• Replace your divots, from tee to green; some courses have a container full of sand and seed on each golf cart; use it to fill in your divots.

• On the green, repair your ball marks and any damage made by your spikes. In fact, it's a great idea to always fix at least one extra ball mark on each green.

- Don't damage the green when you put down the flag stick or your bag. Don't lean on your putter (it could make a dent in the putting surface), and be sure to replace the flag stick properly in the cup before leaving the green.

- Follow the local course rules which explain where you can drive your golf cart.

- When you take practice swings — on the tee or in the fairway — repair any damage you cause (e.g., replace divots).

- Always read the score card for local course information and rules.

- Be sure to observe all signs regarding driving carts, ground under repair, flower beds, cart-paths, safety and other information.

- Pick up your tee after you hit your shot; tees can

  damage golf maintenance equipment.

Etiquette Checklist

1. Courtesy on the course is a priority!

2. Play safe — don't endanger another golfer.

3. Take care of the course.

4. Keep up the proper pace of play.

5. Know golf terminology.

6. Read the back of the scorecard to learn local course rules.

7. Know the basic important rules of golf.

8. Keep a current copy of the USGA Rules Book in your bag.

9. Compliment your fellow golfers on a good shot.

10. Watch the ball when others in your group hit.

11. Don't talk while other players are hitting.

12. Have fun!

Acknowledgments

With many thanks for the support and input from our many golfing friends — especially our "Saturday and Sunday morning groups" at MountainGate Country Club in Los Angeles — Jack Alvarez, Tom Beaver, Julius Coleman, Ron Katz, Dan Kaufmann, Dave Knutson, Bernie Lipps, Norm Miller, Hank Patao, Bernie Rosen and Bob Safford — who have shared their experiences, stories, frustrations and business successes on golf courses around the world. We value the added inspiration and encouragement from Frank Purcell, George Siegel and Roger Rebbun.

Our sincere appreciation goes to Nancy Oliver, founder of the Executive Women's Golf Association (EWG), for her special contribution in authoring *Playing In A Man's World* (Chapter 7), highlighting the opportunities and problems of women as they make their mark on the business world of golf. EWG is a national women's golf organization with more than 13,000 members in 88 chapters throughout the United States.

Rick Connelly & Mark Grody

© 1996

Richard D. Connelly & Mark S. Grody

About The Authors

Rick Connelly is a native Californian who grew up in an entertainment and sports environment. At the age of 13 he started playing golf with his father and business executives. He became a caddie at Bel-Air Country Club in Los Angeles and later became the head starter and caddie-master there.

After college Connelly held several management positions, including 11 years as marketing manager of a Fortune 500 company. For the past several years he has been a consultant to major golf club manufacturers.

His business golf game stays on target with his memberships at Monterey Peninsula Country Club, Pebble Beach, Calif., and MountainGate Country Club, Los Angeles. He maintains a single-digit handicap.

Connelly credits much of his business success to his early upbringing in the entertainment world. His father was a producer, creator and writer of TV shows and films, and his credits included The *Munsters* and *Leave It To Beaver*, the latter of which was inspired by his young son, Ricky.

Mark Grody has been a writer and public relations executive for more than 30 years. During his career, he has created and directed public relations, promotional and marketing communications activities for a number of Fortune 500 companies.

A native of Milwaukee and a journalism/public relations graduate of the University of Wisconsin, he grew up in a sports-oriented family, with his father being the assistant sports editor of the *Milwaukee Sentinel* and his mother an executive with the then Milwaukee Braves major league baseball team.

Grody began his public relations career with General Motors, holding several senior positions throughout the United States. He later founded, built and ran one of the largest public relations agencies in Los Angeles which he sold to an international communications conglomerate several years ago.

He began playing golf as a youngster and keeps his business golf game in tune at MountainGate Country Club, Los Angeles, where he has a single-digit handicap.